This guide is intended to provide information on finding and identifying routes to date in the Hall of Legends and surrounding towers. There maybe inaccuracies regarding the routes or protection and you're welcome to contact me with any concerns.
And, as always,
don't be stupid, climb at your own risk.

ISBN 979-8-9941046-0-6

1
2
3
4
5 6
7 8
9 10
11 12
13 14 15
HALL OF LEGENDS
18 17 16
TONTO TOWER
37
36
35
34
19
USSEN TOWER
20 21
22 23 24
33 32
KNOTTY TOWER
31 30 29
APACHE TOWERS
25 26 27 28
BEAST WALL 38-42
OLD ROAD
PARKING

THE HALL OF LEGENDS

Apache Leap is the towering volcanic cliff band that runs across the eastern skyline above Superior. Nestled in the middle, in the tallest, deepest cleft, is the Hall of Legends. With routes that scatter across the 300-500ft cliff, up both sides of the slot canyon, and on the surrounding towers there's plenty to keep you busy for days. And there's something for everyone! There's many well-bolted, single pitch sport routes, all equipped with mussies at the top, that range in length. But the real gems of the area are the 4-6 pitch routes that sweep up either side of the canyon, each one has an alpine feel but is bolted like a sport route.

Without 4WD, the approach will be long -- whether you hike in from the bottom or the top -- but well worth it. About 45 minutes to an hour will get you to some of the best multipitch sport routes in the state with lots of exposure, fun movement, and a sense of adventure.

GETTING THERE

FROM THE TOP:

From Superior take US-60 east for 4 miles and take a right onto Magma Mine Road. Park at the end of Magma Mine Road (the same parking for the Mine Area), approximately 2 miles from the turn off the highway. Start on the trail for The Mine until you reach the dirt road, follow it up and over the hill toward the mining platform. About halfway down the hill, you'll see cairns and two white posts on your right. If you reach the flat area, you've gone too far.

Once off the dirt road and on the trail, follow cairns carefully. This shouldn't be hard as they're abundant. The trail winds up the backside of the Magma Gardens, crossing the drainage twice, and then turning left once you get close to the crest. Once you turn left, continue over three ridges before turning right again, and continuing up toward the top of the Apache Leap.

If you've stayed on trail, once you reached the top you are standing between Mangas/Coloradas and Victorio. There is a big rock with a bolt on top roughly dead center of these three routes. If you look west, you're looking at the east face of the Ussen tower.

Approximate hiking time is 45 minutes to an hour.

To descend, you have a few options -- some better than others -- depending on which route you're looking to get on. At the top of some of the routes in and surrounding The Hall there is a small rock with the name of the route. In some cases, you can rap the route you want to climb. Even if your chosen route is rappel-able it's recommended, for the routes in The Hall, to walk south (climber's right) toward the narrow end of The Hall where you'll see a large cairn at the top of Naiche and Lozen. Both of these routes will get you to the bottom with two raps. Lozen is a cleaner rappel but Naiche can be done with an 80m for one 40m rap. ALWAYS TIE KNOTS AT THE END OF YOUR

ROPE AS MANY OF THE RAPPELS AT THE LEAP ARE A FULL 35 METERS!

Once you have reached the ground head down the notch (AKA the death gulley) following a loose trail and hand lines. Stay mindful descending and ascending the gulley, there is an abundance of loose rock and a helment is a MUST.

For the routes just outside of the main hall -- Net Positive Impact (NPI) and routes near it -- there is a designated rappel line. It can be done with a 60m rope but, again we emphasize, tie knots in the ends. The rappel line is climber's left of NPI and shares the top anchors with NPI. All anchors on the rappel line, with the exception of the top anchors of NPI, are two bolts with rap rings. If you pass an anchor without rap rings, it's not on the rappel line. Four rappels will place you at the base between NPI, Greatest Sin, and Goyahkla.

Turn off the dirt road at these GPS coordinates: 33.2975263, -111.0698535

The saddle at the halfway point: 33.2920422, -111.0757202

Your rough destination: 33.2860880, -111.0759613

NPI area: 33.2869709, -111.0763462

If you're looking for the easiest climb out of The Hall, Naiche's Escape is a single pitch 5.8.
If climbing becomes not an option and you would like to hike out, you can follow the eastern side of the canyon all the way back up to the rim. Alternatively, you can hike down to town and try your luck getting a ride back to your car. But neither of these are an easy jaunt and more so options in the case of an emergency that has rendered climbing an impossibility.

FROM THE BOTTOM:

The approach from the bottom requires a 4WD, high clearance vehicle.
From US-60/AZ-177 intersection, take the 177 for 0.5 miles and hook a left on the dirt road straight across from Sunset Drive. Fair warning, the road is rough -- though, if we all stop a few times on the way up and toss loose or big rocks out of the way it will inevitably get better. There are several large pull-offs along the way and if you reach a point you don't want to continue past, park at one of these.
At the very end of the road is a large, flat parking area. From the parking area, walk back down the road about a 100 yards and directly below the lowest tower you'll find cairns and a dirt trail heading up toward The Hall.

THINGS YOU'LL NEED

No one should have to say pack the obvious things like water, snacks, a harness, etc. so just use a little common sense but for the more specific things to get you up and down:

a 70m rope
20 draws
a helmet
& even if it's a nice, sunny day it's a good idea to bring a jacket

SUGGESTIONS

WEATHER AND WIND

The Hall of Legends is a winter crag. Most of the cliff band gets sun majority of the day, making it a great spot for the colder days but even on warmer days you'll find that the east facing side of the Ussen tower will stay shady and cold.

As always, check the weather before heading out but keep in mind that even on a warm day The Hall can feel a lot colder once you rap down in even if it's a beautiful day up top and it's a good idea to always pack a jacket.

If it's been raining heavily, give the rock a day or so to dry out -- as it is, the rock can be soft and friable and the water won't help.

And as well as checking the weather, it's a good idea to check the wind direction. If the wind is coming from the east you can expect a nice, calm day on the cliff. (Even strong winds, if they're coming from the east, you won't feel.) If it's coming from the west however, know that you might have a rather rough day up there.

CAMPING

Camping near The Hall of Legends is completely free. The Oak Flat Campground, about 4 miles away from the trailhead, has a multitude of individual campsites and many have a picnic table and a firepit with a grill. Regularly maintained outhouses are also posted at the campground as well. There is a 14 day stay limit enforced by the USFS.

WATER & FOOD

The nearest water source is down in Superior. For filling up reusable water containers your best bet is the Save Money Market on Main Street. Alternatively, the Circle K has a water refill station that works sometimes.

The Save Money Market is also the best place to go nearby for groceries but if you're looking for more of a selection you'll have to make the 20 mile trip up to Globe.

As for eating out after a long day of climbing, you'll be able to find a nice little selection down in town between Silver King, Jalapenos, and Porters.

GOYAHKLA 1

Geronimo was born Goyahkla (One Who Yawns) and was known for his spiritual leadership and tenacity in battle -- the latter of which is speculated to have earned him the given name Geronimo (Spanish for Jerome) as Mexican soldiers he fought against were known to call out to Saint Jerome for help.

THE SCOOP

This climb follows the center of an amazing 400 foot ever narrowing rib to the top of Apache Leap

P1 (5.9) Shares the same first pitch with Greatest Sin. Start right of blocky chimney -- the first two bolts are the trickiest! but avoid bailing left into the chimney. Traverse right below the first bolt and then stick to the right of the bolt line.Climb to ledge then up ever narrowing pillar full of, some unexpectedly, sinker pockets. 35m 15 bolts. (This is the last pitch you can bail on with one rope!)

P2 (5.8) Continue straight up the narrow rib for 15 bolts. If the first bolt looks high, fear not, once you start climbing you'll find yourself at it in just a few easy moves whether you stick to the right or left side of the rib. Then traverse slightly left through some fun moves on the face to the anchors. A slightly extended anchor here lets you belay from a stem between the face and the top of the pillar climber's left (facing out towards the incredible view).

Pitch 3 (5.8) Short but fun! Continue up the face to juggy ledges to the top past 5 more bolts to the top.

FA: Jason Conlon, Cas Sundell

GREATEST SIN 2

Named in honor of words spoken by the Apache Activist Wendsler Nosie Sr. regarding our mistreatment of Mother Earth.

THE SCOOP

P1 (5.9) Shares first pitch with Goyahkla. At the anchors, look climber's right for your bolt line (Goyahkla continues straight up the fin). 15 bolts.

P2 (5.10c) Step across a gap to the main face! Exposed but well protected. Steep climbing on great rock and pockets, past a

thoughtful crux, leads to a belay stance that's hiding just out of sight until you're almost right on top of it. 18 bolts.

P3 (5.9) Straight up on pockets, jams and lieback cracks for 6 bolts to the top. Shares anchors with the top pitch of NPI.

FA: Charlie Brown, Dave Gunn, Ian Gunn

NET POSITIVE IMPACT (NPI) 3

In the environmental impact statement from Resolution Copper, they claim that the copper mining project in Queen Creek will have a "net positive impact" on the water future of Arizona. With even a tiny bit of critical thought, one can understand that this is simply impossible. Tug at the threads of the impact statement, and you'll find it unraveling rather quickly. This route exists to show what a "net positive impact" might actually look like. A great day out on moderate terrain, well protected, established by a wholesome community of lifelong climbers that would prefer we not blow the place into a 2000ft toxic crater.

-Note from the first ascensionists

THE SCOOP

P1 (5.7) Starts just left of a hand crack. The line trends up and left at the beginning, then straightens out up to the belay station. If you're thinking it looks a little runout from the second bolt, fear not! There's a bolt hiding just out of view. 7 bolts.

P2 (5.7) Step up and right into a flaring chimney, climb as it widens and eventually commit to face climbing moves to climbers left. A few reachy moves here, but it's full of great edges and well-bolted. Can be linked with P1. 8 bolts.

P3 (5.7) The MONEY. Follow a column-like feature to a roof, and pull on through. Can feel pretty wild. Save a bit of gas in the tank for some smaller (but very positive) holds above. 13 bolts.

P4 (5.7) Reward yourself with a lower-angle cruise and top out at another set of bolts with chains. Can be linked with P3, recommended to extend some clips if doing so. 9 bolts.

FA: Dave Gunn, Ian Gunn

DESCENT

Use the designated rappel line (climber's left of NPI) for these routes. Goyahkla and Greatest Sin cannot be rapped with one rope.

DAHTESTE 4

Dahteste was a skilled warrior and linguist; fluent in her native tongue as well as English and Spanish. She was a valued translator, mediator, and messenger for the Apache bands she rode with and the US Calvary. Her family joined with Geronimo's band after their final escape from San Carlos, at which time her and Lozen became close companions and remained good friends for the rest of their lives. After Geronimo's surrender in 1886, and the coinciding betrayal of the agreed upon treaty by the US government, Dahteste was held at Fort Marion in Florida as a prisoner of war with the rest of the Chiricahua Apache for 8 years before being relocated to Fort Sill, Oklahoma. After 27 years of internment, the government gave 300 Chiricahuas the choice to remain in Fort Sill or move to the Mescalero Apache Reservation. She chose the later, moving to Whitetail, where she lived well into her 90s. She passed away in 1955, outliving her friend, Lozen, by 65 years and, according to Eve Ball, "Dahteste, to the end of her life, mourned Lozen."

THE SCOOP

(5.11b) This is a single pitch, rap-in route located on a peninsula of rock between Mangas and NPI. This is a rap-in-climb-out route that does not reach the base of The Hall. Very important to note that an 80m rope, or two ropes, is required to make the rappel!
Despite any extra trouble you might have to go through to get to the base of the route, it's well worth doing. Once you reach the ledge at the bottom, follow the bolts back up an ever steepening face over buldges to a roof (avoid choss above by crimping and underclinging right out to jugs). After pulling the roof, cruise to the anchors.

FA: Aaron Peterson

MANGAS 5

Mangas Coloradas, also known as Dasoda-hae (Red Sleeves), chief of the Eastern Chiricahua Apache, was known as a suberb warrior and leader. Despite being known as a champion in one-to-one combat and a genius military tactician, for many years he sought to create peace, not war, with the whites. But tensions grew as settlers continued pushing into Apache land -- staking homesteads and grazing livestock, developing mines, antagonizing Apache people and more often than not, killing the native people when and wherever they got the chance. The possibility of peace was destroyed in 1861 when the US military led Cochise, another renown Chiricahua chief and Mangas's son-in-law, and his family along with several of his warriors into a trap. Although Cochise managed to escape, his family was held captive and the military torpedoed any negotiations. A bloody fight ensued, known as the Bascom Affair, resulting in the death of several Apache warriors who were strung up from ropes in trees. This event was the catalyst for an all-out war that Mangas fought alongside Cochise and Geronimo for the next three years.
In1863, US troops flew a white flag at Pinos Altos and under the pretense

of negotiating peace Mangas responded, hopeful to end the war that he felt had been forced upon his people. The military had no intentions of negotiating peace, however, flying the flag only as a ruse and captured then later executed and mutilated the chief.
This, of course, was met with anger and even more retaliation from the Apache and the war continued for the next nine years.

THE SCOOP

Currently the furthest left bolt line in The Hall.

P1 (5.10b) Begin on a steep but juggy lieback past a tricky buldge to technical face climbing, a fun, little crux to a giant hueco belay. 25 meters.

P2 (5.10a) Climb out the overhanging left side of the hueco on jugs. Continue on even more jugs, past the big ledge, to the belay ledge with two anchors. The left set is for Mangas, the right set is for Coloradas. 20 meters.

P3 (5.10a) This amazing pitch starts right away with thoughtful crack climbing. Continue for a full 35 meters of fun face and crack to the crux towards the end before pulling over onto the belay ledge on the north face.

P4 (5.10a) Traverse left then directly up on solid rock, pull a superb overhang before cruising to the summit. 25 meters.

FA: Charlie Brown, Jason Conlon

COLORADAS 6

THE SCOOP

Coloradas is a variation to the last two pitches of Mangas. Start from the right set of anchors at the top of P2.

P1 (5.10b) Amazing, but thoughtful and sometimes thin, face to cracks and overhangs to a belay in a hueco. Trust your feet and try not to get too sucked into the large crack in the dihedral.

P2 (5.10a) Climb through and out of the hueco and into the overhang, then straight up the face to the top!

FA: Charlie Brown, Jason Conlon

STANDING IN FRONT OF THE ENEMY 7

The Bedonkohe-Nde-nda-he [Standing in Front of the Enemy People], was a local group of Bedonkohe who allied with relatives of the Nednhi band. The principal leader of the Nednhi was 'Tan-din-bil-no-jui' [He Who Brings Many Things with Him], known as Juh.

THE SCOOP

Just downhill from the start of Victorio.

P1 (5.10c) Start up the broken overhangs to a series of liebacks on jugs then transition onto the thin face for two bolts before moving back onto great holds and a hand crack to the good belay ledge. 12 bolts.

P2 (5.8) Easily combined with P1 if you so please. Easy face climbing on jugs with one thoughful move out left down low. Mostly super fun, steep pocket-pulling.

P3 (5.10a) Climb up in the alcove and stem across to a big jug, past a hand crack, and traverse left toward the arete. Mostly climbs the arete. Make sure to look around the corner for a few moves, before moving back right toward the end. Big, fun moves on the steep face deposit you at the anchors in the hueco. (Anchor shared with Coloradas).

P4 (5.10d) Of the two bolt lines leaving the P3 anchors, the right line is yours. Start up the slab to a series of incredible, airy overhangs all the way to the summit. Hands down the money pitch.

FA: Charlie Brown, Cas Sundell

JUH 8

Juh was a highly successful warrior and leader of the Nednai Apaches as well as a cousin of Geronimo. He led serveral raids and fought alongside Mangas Coloradas, Victorio, Geronimo, and Cochise.

THE SCOOP

(5.11c) Alternate start to P1 of Standing in Front of the Enemy and starts a few yards uphill to the right of the original line on a good three finger pocket under a small roof. Stay off the right wall and pop up to the rail and then pull around the corner. Follow the clean face until reaching the steep crux. Pull the small roof onto the belay ledge. 10 bolts.

FA: Charlie Brown, Cas Sundell

VICTORIO 9

Born in 1809, Victorio grew up surrounded by hositility between the natives of the southwest and the encroaching white and Mexican settlers which bred a determination to resist the loss of his homeland. In his twenties, he began to ride with Geronimo, Nana, and other Apache leaders on raids in the northern Mexico area and by 1862 it's said that he had joined forces with Mangas Coloradas. Following the death of Mangas, Victorio emerged as a leader -- forming a band of roughly 300. US officers, that he fought against, regarded him as a strong leader and tactician. But after nearly a decade of battle and evading capture, he was convinced to accept resettlement of his people to the land near San Carlos. It wasn't long before they decided that the reservation was unacceptable -- with temperatures reaching 110° making farming next to impossible -- and Victorio moved his people to Ojo Caliente, effectively making him, once again, an outlaw in the eyes of the US. Not long after, the army forced most of the Apache people back to San Carlos but Victorio and around 150 of his people eluded capture, disappearing into the desert for the next two years where they survived by ambushing and raiding US troops and Mexican and US sheepherders.

It wasn't until 1880 that he was tracked down to an area just south of El Paso, TX where Mexican soldiers killed all but 17 of the trapped Apaches. Although the exact manner in which Victorio died is unclear. In some accounts, Victorio took his own life rather than surrender. Though there are other stories in which he was killed by the troops. Regardless of how, his death made him a martyr and only strengthened the determination among others to continue the fight.

THE SCOOP

Victorio was the first route bolted in The Hall.

P1 (5.8+) This pitch shares the first bolts with Apache Wolf but splits left before the first roof. Start in the offwidth up to a ledge, then cut left. The crux of this pitch is a slightly awkward squeeze in the chimney off the ledge but it's very well protected and you're rewarded with fun climbing above. Be aware that it can be easy to wander onto the route next door so stay on the left bolt line to keep your grade.

P2 (5.8+) Start out the left side of the belay on sustained but fun face moves. When you reach the small arete, stick to the left (clipping bolts out right) and before the top of the arete start moving back out right along a tip-toe traverse ledge (airy and fun!) then up twin cracks to the belay on a small tower.

P3 (5.7) The airy fun continues! Move around the exposed arete to the right of the belay and follow it up as it evolves into a steep, juggy face. When you reach the overhang, head up and left then cruise to the anchors.

FA: Charlie Brown, Jason Conlon

APACHE WOLF 10

Victorio was also known by the name Apache Wolf.

THE SCOOP

P1 (5.10b) Shares the first two bolts with Victorio but then cuts up and right over an electrifying 4ft roof, the definite crux of the first pitch. After the roof the pitch backs off a little as you head up the face with a few crack moves thrown in here or there, though it remains strenuous. Climb past the anchors for Victorio P1 to another belay station 20ft up.

Coloradas (orange), Mangas (green), Standing in Front of the Enemy (blue), Victorio (pink), Apache Wolf (yellow)

P2 (5.10c) Start up the face left of the belay to a crack. Pull fun, exciting moves up the crack until it thins and finally disappears. A few tricky moves following this connect up to the last 5 bolts of P2 of Victorio.

P3 (5.7) Same last pitch as Victorio.

FA: Charlie Brown, Jason Conlon, Cas Sundell

GOUYEN 11

Gouyen ("The One Who Is Wise") was revered for her courage. Her legacy began in the early 1870's after her first husband was murdered and scalped in front of her during a Comanche raid. Her culture calls for vengeance as a matter of honor though, in this case, there was no one in her family to avenge her husband (her father-in-law too old and any other male relatives too weak). So, following a mourning period and determined to settle the score, she snuck out of camp, packing only food, water, and her beaded dress from her Sunrise Ceremony. After four nights of traveling on foot she came to the Comanche camp where they were enthralled in their victory dance. She changed into her ceremonial dress and slunk toward the fire, joining the throngs of drunken dancers. Over the course of the night, she approached the cheif, still wearing her husband's scalp on his belt, lured him into the dance with her and then eventually into the shadows outside of camp. Still weapon-less, when he pulled her close she sunk her teeth into his neck and refused to let go until she crushed his throat. Then, using his knife, cut his heart out and took several trophies before stealing his horse to ride back home.

Later, she remarried and her and her husband joined Victorio's band. When the band was ambushed near El Paso among the 17 to escape were Gouyen and her husband and son. When she was inevitably sent to the San Carlos Reservation she was among those who escaped with Geronimo in 1883, joining his band for the last battles of the Apache Wars. Following their surrender three years later, she was taken as a prisoner of war and died at Fort Sill in 1903.

THE SCOOP

(5.10b) Just downhill from Lozen and right above the chockstone tunnel. This is a full 70m rope length (although it can be easily broken into two pitches by moving right halfway through and using the Lozen anchors) of crimps, seams, jugs, and cracks. Start on jugs and the large crack and head up, wandering right, before traversing back left to the reachy crux. From here it mellows as you move up and left around a corner into a chimney (though you're best off climbing the face) up to the anchors shared with Lozen. 21 bolts.

FA: Aaron Peterson, Cas Sundell

LOZEN 12

Lozen ("Dextrous Horse Theif") was born in the early 1840s into the band of Chiricahua Apache led by her older brother Victorio, who would later regard her as his right hand. She learned to ride a horse at the age of seven and by an early age she was not only one of the best riders in the band but an incredible marksman, incredible with a knife, and a renowned military strategist. She quickly became a well respected warrior. Single women weren't typically allowed to ride with raiding parties but, with every top warrior wanting her at their side, an exception was made. She is noted not only for her skill as a warrior but also remembered for being a powerful medicine woman, Shaman, and seer -- often predicting not only when enemy parties were close but discerning direction and distance.

In her life, Lozen fought along side Victorio, Cochise, Mangas Coloradas, Geronimo,Naiche, Nana, and others and, according to Peter Aleshire's book, fought in more campaigns than the renowned leaders. In 1886, when the surrender of the remaining Apache resistance was negotiated, Geronimo and his band agreed to a two year exile in Florida -- though the US government never had intentions of allowing them to return to their homeland. The camps that they were sent to were not only overcrowded but filthy, disease-ridden, and malnutrution ran rampant. Lozen died as a prisoner of war at one of these camps in Alabama on June 17, 1889.

THE SCOOP

Lozen is the second to last set of anchors from the (climber's) right on the west side of The Hall. Starts next to a small tree.

P1 (5.10b) Start on jugs that lead to a steep, pumpy crack. Ride the crack for a while as it trends up and right but keep your eye on the bolt line! Eventually, break out of the crack and onto the face following crimps and jugs to the anchor.

P2 (5.10b) Head out right and up a fun overhang to a juggy flake, then cruise to the anchors.

FA: Charlie Brown, Cas Sundell

NAICHE 13

Naiche ("Mischief Maker"), son of Cochise, was the last hereditary leader of the Chiricahua Apache. He was at the head of many raids in Arizona and in 1885 escaped the San Carlos Reservation with Geronimo. Soon after, in 1886, Naiche and his followers were captured, imprisioned, and over the next few years he was moved from fort to fort. It wasn't until 1913 that Naiche was able to return to the southwest where he lived the rest of his life, the next six years, on the Mescalero Reservation in New Mexico.

THE SCOOP

Can be done in one, long pitch (recommended to use runners or back clean some of the early bolts) or broken up into two using the intermediate anchor on Naiche's Escape. Nachie starts just up the hill from Lozen, the bolt line a few yards below the chockstone.

(5.10d) Begin underneath the roof and climb up and right, following a series of pumpy, airy, and extremely fun overhangs to face climbing that eases off the higher you get. 19 bolts.

FA: Charlie Brown, Jason Conlon

NAICHE'S ESCAPE 14

This is the furthest (climber's) right route in The Hall. Start from behind the giant chockstone.

(5.8) Climb up onto the chockstone to clip the first bolt. Follow the face 40m to the top. Can be done in one or two pitches. 17 bolts.

FA: Charlie Brown, Andy Melancon

MISCHIEF MAKER 15

This route starts on a bushy ledge halfway down the Naiche rappels. Cannot be accessed from the bottom of the gulley (without climbing); rap-in-climb-out route.

(5.9) From the ledge follow the right bolt line over a small roof and continue up fun face-climbing to the Naiche anchors. (It is also possible to climb the second half of Naiche from the same ledge. Climb the left bolt line at 5.6). 9 bolts.

FA: Charlie Brown

WEST SIDE OF THE HALL

The east-facing wall of The Hall is steep and almost always shady and dry -- the very top gets just a little sun in the mornings.

If approaching from the bottom, hike to the top of the gulley -- when the trail splits, follow the handlines right. If approaching from the top, rap in on Naiche or Lozen, follow the trail down, pass through the hole beneath the chockstone, and after you round the next corner continue straight across the gulley and back uphill slightly.

CHILD OF WATER 16

Child of Water is one of the two sons of the Apache god Ussen.

Child of Water is the furthest left bolt line on the east face of The Hall.

THE SCOOP

P1 (5.9) Starts in a steep dihedral with good holds. From the first big ledge, traverse out left, then up to a comfortable belay ledge. Anchors for Child of Water are the furthest left, closest to the small dihedral.

P2 (5.11) Hands down, the money pitch -- long, steep, and fun! Start up the corner to a face, then traverse right on crimps to a small overhang. A short traverse back left then head straight up for a few more bolts. (Traversing allll the way back left to the corner up high lessens the grade.) Finishes out right on underclings and steep liebacking to the belay ledge. Can be combined with P1 and still reach the ground with a 70m, but it's close.

P3 (5.10c) Start out right before traversing back left through an overhang. Short but steep! Finish with a mantle up to the chains.

FA: Charlie Brown, Blythe Allers

SLAYER OF MONSTERS 17

Slayer of Monsters is one of the two sons of the Apache god Ussen.

THE SCOOP

A variation to P2 of Child of Water. When you reach the first belay ledge, traverse over to the middle set of anchors.

(5.12c) Start with liebacking and compressing before transitioning into the crack up to the roof. Undercling out the buldge and deadpoint on incut crimps through the crux. Stays on you till the very end, so find rests where you can!

FA: Charlie Brown

SONS OF USSEN 18

"It was on White Mountain, according to legend, that White Painted Woman gave birth to two sons, Child of Water and Killer of Enemies [Slayer of Monsters]. They were born during a turbulent rainstorm when thunder and lighting came from the sky. Giant Monsters who wanted to kill them feared White Painted Woman and her sons, whom she raised to be brave and skilled. When they grew up to be men, they rose up and killed the monsters of the earth. There was peace and all human beings were saved."[1]

THE SCOOP

A variation to P2 of Child of Water. When you reach the first belay ledge traverse right, past the anchors for Slayer of Monsters, to the furthest right set of anchors.

(5.12b) An airy start, traverse to the right off the belay ledge and head up the steep, bulging face with a good mix of liebacking and underclinging in the cracks interrupted by sections of crimpy face climbing. Powerful and delicate at the finish.

FA: Charlie Brown

USSEN 19

"The chief deity of the Chiricahua Apache was Ussen, whose will governed all. Ussen existed before the creation of the universe. He created the first Mother with no parents who sang four times. Her singing began the creation of the universe. Ussen also created the first Boy and Sun God who shook hands. The sweat from this handshake created the Earth. The Earth was small at first, so they kicked it around and it gained mass like a snowball rolling down a hill, getting larger and larger. Ussen also created Tarantula, who increased the Earth's size even more by pulling on it with four cords of web which he spun. Ussen then created the first people and fire and then he left. Ussen continues to watch events unfold from afar and still intercedes from time to time." [2]

THE SCOOP

Ussen is the prominent arete of the fin that creates the west side of the hall. If approaching from the bottom, follow the trail up from the dirt road and just at the mouth of the gulley there will be a fainter trail to your right. It's a small scramble up to the base of the route. If approaching from the top, rap in and follow the handlines all the way down the gulley. The start of the route will be to your left just after the last set of handlines.

P1 (5.9) Start up the broken face at the back of the small gulley. The first few bolts take you through blocks, and eventually cracks, before trending climber's left to a ledge. From the ledge clip a bolt and head up the face left of the bolt line, gradually trasitioning into liebacks that ease off the higher you get until pulling over onto the final, big ledge of the first pitch to the anchors.

P2 (5.8) Before starting the second pitch, you'll have to climb down slightly and traverse climber's left across the large ledge (possibly through a bit of light vegetation) to the belay station. Follow the bolt line up through blocky rock to a tricky move (if it looks run out, fear not, there's a bolt hiding from you). From here, the pitch only gets cleaner and more fun.

P3 (5.10a) Start up the easy, slab-angled terrain on big holds to a roof. Work into the dihedral below the roof before pulling up and over onto the pocketed face. Anchor in at the top of the spire and start eyeing the next pitch across the gap. (Can be linked with P2)
Note that this is the last good place to bail if you so please. And if you do, note that you'd be robbing yourself of some serious fun.

P4 (5.8) This pitch starts on the other side of the gap. If you already know how to set up a lower-out on a bite, feel free to skip on down a few sentences. If not, read on.
If it sounds complicated in theory, fear not, it's not in practice. And you can look up videos of how to do so online as well.

Leading the pitch:

- *There's a bolt above and slightly left of the P3 anchors with a quicklink attached. Hang a draw on this bolt and clip in the rope like normal, then lower into the gap between the two pillars.*
- *At the bottom, tip-toe your way across the chockstone and start up the face.*
- *Once you've clipped a few bolts -- however many you're comfortable with, but recommended to do this before you get too high -- take, lower down, and back clean at least the first bolt, if not the first two to alieviate the rope drag. (Note that it wouldn't hurt to take the draws with you when you back clean.)*

What you're looking for here is a rope that swoops across the gap from the anchors of P3 to the face on P4, instead of a rope that goes down from the anchors before going up the face.

- *When you reach the P4 anchors, go in direct, let your follower know to take you off belay, and then resist the urge to start pulling up the rope like normal.*

Following the pitch:

- *Once you've taken the leader off belay and while you're still in direct, tie yourself in short on a bite on a locker.*
- *Let the leader know to put you on belay and take up whatever small amount of slack is in the system.*

•Untie your original figure 8 and thread the non-working side of the rope through the quicklink on the single bolt that's up and left of the P3 anchors (you should have roughly 100 ft of rope to work with).
•Pull out your belay device and put yourself on belay on the non-working side of the rope.
•Clean the P3 anchor and then lower yourself across the gap. Ideally, there's a few moments where you'll find yourself airbone between the two pillars.
•Once you're across the gap you can take yourself off belay, pull the end of the rope out of the quicklink, and start your way up the pitch with the leader belaying as normal.
This pitch follows the blocky face, through a few cracks, to a thoughtful final bolt before the belay ledge.

P5 (5.7) Your first bolt may be hiding from you just slightly but as soon as you start to make your way up and left it will come into sight. Continue around the left arete of the tower onto the east face. Continue up the the key terrain feature that defines this line. It's a pitch of incredible stemming inside a near-perfect dihedral.

P6 (5.10b/c) A start that can feel airy! Big feet and small hands lead up and left to a crux -- thinking long and tall thoughts here couldn't hurt -- and then over an easy but dramatic mantle move. From there, it's a cruise to the anchors.

FA: Charlie Brown, Dave Gunn

Child of Water, Slayer of Monsters, Sons of Ussen, Ussen

DESCENT FOR ROUTES ON THE USSEN TOWER

Three raps with a 60m and it *can* be done in two raps with a 70m -- but it's important to note the emphasis on the 'can'. ***The second rap is close and not all 70s are created equal, tie knots in your rope***, and if you haven't already done it in two raps and know you make it or you want to play it on the safe side, descend in three.

Rap the east face straight below the last anchor to a large ledge. Then rap down Child of Water (the furthest left anchor on the ledge) either to the ground (swing climber's left, aim for the large pedastal at the base of Child of Water) or to the P1 anchors and rap a third time. Walk down the gulley and to your packs.

SINGLE PITCH ROUTES ON THE USSEN TOWER

White Hactcin, Black Hactcin, Gaan, Magazu, and Nilo are all located at the base of the Ussen tower. Easiest to access approaching from the bottom. From the road, head up the trail to a platform below the death gulley. If you're approaching from the top, rap Naiche or Lozen and follow the gulley all the way down to the end of the handlines.

WHITE HACTCIN 20

In the beginning there was nothing - no earth, no living beings. There were only darkness, water, and Cyclone, the wind. There were no humans, but only the Hactcin... The Hactcin made the earth, the underworld beneath it, and the sky above it.[3]

THE SCOOP

Located on the NW facing wall just outside of the alcove at the base of Ussen. White and Black Hactcin share the first few and last few bolts.

(5.11a/b) Start up the chimney to the crack. When the crack ends, the routes split. White Hactcin shoots out left, up a steep face to underclings. Continue pulling left on jugs before heading up over the bulge to gain the thin arete. Following a technical face crux, pull onto a ledge. From there, it's easy climbing to the anchors. 20 bolts.

FA: Charlie Brown, Ben Ramsey, Soren Staursbol

BLACK HACTCIN 21

THE SCOOP

(5.10d) Shares the same start as White Hactcin. When the routes split, head up and right on pockets to a reach with high feet then start to move up the dihedral. Follow it for as long as you can before moving back left to join with White Hactcin on the rest ledge. 20 bolts.

FA: Charlie Brown, Soren Staursbol

GAAN 22

The Gaan are mountain spirits.

THE SCOOP

Gaan is the furthest left route on the face at the base of the Ussen tower.

(5.11a) Start up the crack; jams, to lieback, and eventually make your way onto the face. A few thin moves lead to a good rest, then head left on an undercling and overhanging jugs. Classic Queen Creek vertical face climbing leads to one more good rest and, eventually, the anchors. 20 bolts.

FA: Charlie Brown, Ben Ramsey, Andy Melancon

MAGAZU 23

Mağážu - Apache for rain.

THE SCOOP

Boltline just to the right of Gaan.

(5.11b) Start on the large platform. Head up the face for a few bolts, toward the obvious large flake. Move up on crimps, trending right, before heading back left on a small ledge. Continue up the face to a small roof with jugs. If you like old-school, thin, technical face climbing -- this is the route for you! 20 bolts.

FA: Carl Leon

NILO 24

Níló, meaning hail.

THE SCOOP

Furthest right bolt line on the face at the base of the Ussen tower.

(5.10 b/c) Start off the platform at the base and cruise up to the crux roughly halfway up the route. From there, look forward to sustained climbing to the anchors. 18 bolts.

FA: Carl Leon, Josh Fellman

APACHE TOWERS

The Apache Towers are the first two towers that you encounter on the trail once leaving the old road if you're approaching from the bottom. The lower tower is the first large platform you reach on the trail, the upper tower is just up the trail past the first set of steps. (33.2860516, -111.0779173)
If you're approaching from the top, rap in on the designated rappel line near NPI and follow the trail down.

The Apaches referred to themselves as Diné or Inde, meaning 'the people'. The name Apache most likely originated from the Zuñi word apachu, *meaning 'enemy', or potentially the Ute name for the Apaches,* Awa'tehe.

LOWER APACHE TOWER

DO'A 25

Do'a - Apache for first.

THE SCOOP

Furthest left route on the lower Apache tower.

(5.7) Start in the chimney, follow it all the way up to the top of the block. Reach across the gap to clip a bolt before stepping across and pulling up on jugs. Follow the flaring dihedral to the anchors.

FA: Dave Gunn, Charlie Brown, Cas Sundell

LIPAN 26

The Lipan were the indigenous people of what is now Texas. The social unit of the Lipan, as well as the Mescalero, Apaches was the extended family. Several extended families generally formed a group and stayed together, a prominent member acting as chief advisor, and a number of these groups lived in close proximity, able to unite for defensive purposes or social occasions.

THE SCOOP

(5.9) Climb up to a small ledge, through a dihedral, and over a small roof. Staying left on the face over the second roof and the prow keeps you on great 5.9 edges (moving over right into the gulley and away from the bolt line bumps it down to 5.7).

FA: Cheryl Bever, David Everett

YAVAPAI 27

The Yavapai were semi-nomadic hunter-gathers, living and traveling in small groups around the Verde Valley and Oak Creek Canyon. They are linguistically and culturally unrelated to the Apache, though they were often mistakenly referred to as 'Mohave-Apache' by American settlers.

THE SCOOP

(5.9) Starts on the same block ledge as Lipan and moves up the center of the lower Apache tower (the left of the two center bolt lines). Follow jugs up to a small roof just below the anchor.

FA: Unknown

COYOTERO 28

A division of the Apache people, geographically divided into the Pinal Coyoteros and the White Mountain Coyoteros -- groups of both ranging throughout the limits of present day Arizona and western New Mexico. The name Coyoteros originated from the Spanish, meaning 'wolf-men', probably applied on account of their roving habit and suriving via gathering and hunting rather than agriculture.

THE SCOOP

(5.9) Start up the same block as Yavapai, clipping the first bolt below the ledge. The second bolt is close to the route on the left but when you reach the third bolt stay right and continue straight up the steep face, then follow the crack up to a ledge. A few more moves lead to a final crux, then the anchors.

FA: Cheryl Bevers

UPPER APACHE TOWER

CHIRACAHUA 29

The Chiricahua Apache belong to a southern group of Athabaskan people, originating in northwestern North America. Comprised of several different Apache bands, they entered into the southwest somewhere between 1400-1500 and while they settled in present-day SE Arizona, SW New Mexico, and northern Mexico they maintained a fairly nomadic lifestyle, spending winter on the plains and summer in the mountains.

THE SCOOP

Farthest left line on the upper tower. Only line on the south-facing wall.

(5.9) Start directly below the first bolt on steep terrain with incut edges. Pass a small crux low down and continue up fun, vertical climbing to a bulge and the second crux. Toward the top, start trending left, hugging the arete.

FA: Charlie Brown, John Mudd, Dave Gunn

MESCALERO 30

Nomadic hunter-gathers dwelling throughout the Southwest in present day Texas, Arizona, Chihuahua and Sonora, Mexico. Today, three sub-tribes, Mescalero, Lipan and Chiricahua make up the Mescalero Apache Tribe.

THE SCOOP

The center line on the upper tower.

(5.9) Start on steep jugs and continue up on a variety of holds, over a small roof, to the top of the tower. Take your rests where you can find them on the way up!

FA: Unknown

JICARILLA 31

The Jicarilla Apache led a semi-nomadic existence in the Sangre de Cristo Mountains and the plains of current day sourthern Colorado and northern New Mexico. They referred to themselves as Haisndayin 'people who came from below' as they believed themselves to be the descendants of the first people to emerge from the underworld. The name jicarilla 'little basket' comes from Mexican-Spanish and referred to the small, sealed baskets they used as flasks.

THE SCOOP

(5.8) Start to the right of Mescalero, slightly up the slope. A short climb on big holds and a nice warm up for the other routes on the tower.

FA: Unknown

KNOTTY TOWER

If you're approaching from the bottom, take the left fork in the trail just past the Upper Apache Tower and follow the rough trail uphill.
If you're approaching from the top, rap the designated rappel line next to NPI and follow the trail down just past the Tonto Tower.
(33.2864444, -111.0772500)

KNOTTY GIRL 32

(5.8) The left variation to the orignal line on the tower. Start up on good holds and head into a small dihedral. A little heady working out of the dihedral around the corner, but once you're on the ledge it's moderate to the next bolt.

FA: Soren Staursbol

KNOTTY TOWER 33

(5.9+) Rightmost line on the tower, black bolts. Good holds lead to a thin and thoughtful crux in the middle then a secure topout. 5 bolts.

FA: David Rozul, Soren Staursbol

FORSTEN 34

(5.6) Located on a small buttress on the right side of the gulley just above the Knotty Tower. A few close bolts lead to a small ledge, then up the slab to the anchors.

FA: Soren Staursbol

TONTO TOWER

From the bottom follow the trail up past the Apache Towers. Once you pass the Knotty Tower, continue uphill on the trail for a few hundred more feet (head in the direction of NPI).
From the top, rap in on the designated rappel line next to NPI. The Tonto Tower is the first tower below the base of NPI and a short scramble down will get you there. (33.2866906, -111.0769265)

COCHINAY 35

Cochinay was a Tonto Apache leader who's people, in 1873, were forcibly moved to the San Carlos Reservation along with several other groups -- a consolidation comprising of upwards of 1,500 people. Tensions ran high in the overcrowded, poorly located reservation and they came to a head on May 27 when US Lieutenant Almy was shot and killed on the reservation. During the commotion that ensued Cochinay, along with leaders Chunz and Chan-deisi, fled with their people. When General Crook learned of the incident he was furious and insisted that no one that had fled would be allowed to surrender until Chunz, Chan-deisi, and Cochinay were brought to San Carlos, dead or alive. Crook placed a heavy bounty on each one of them in hopes that their own people would turn them over for the reward. Several units were immediately dispatched to find them but none were successful in catching up to any of the leaders. By the end of 1873 none of the three leaders had been captured and the names of two more leaders -- Delshay and Eskiminzin -- were added to Crook's list. Just a few months after fleeing the reservation, however, Eskiminzin returned with what remained of his band. They were tired and nearly starved and offered to surrender. Crook however had become increasingly frustrated with the elusive chiefs and decided to take a new, surprisingly brutal approach; refusing to accept their surrender until they brought in the heads of certain chiefs. Within a few months, all four were dead. Cochinay was captured and killed near Tucson on May 26, 1874.

THE SCOOP

(5.12a) A low first bolt leads to a small dihedral. Work your way up and out of it on cool pockets then pull a small buldge to a good rest. Thin moves off the rest lead to the tehcnical crux followed by another opportunity to squeeze another rest in before powering up the last few bolts, past the red point crux, to the anchors. 15 bolts.

FA: Cas Sundell, Charlie Brown

RED ANT 36

Delshay, also known as Red Ant, was a Tonto Apache chief of a tribe in the Mazaztal Mountains during the mid to late 1800s. Throughout the early 1860s the band engaged in raids against the settlers but in 1868 Delshay sought peace and they settled at Camp McDowell along the Verde River where they stayed until 1871 when, following the Camp Grant Massacre, Delshay requested relocation as violence against the Apache's rose.

Despite intial peace after relocating, violence and tensions between the band and settlers led to an intervention by the US Army in 1873 at the request of settlers in the area. On April 25, Delshay's camp on the upper Canyon Creek was located and surrounded and after only the first few shots were fired Delshay raised a white flag. Their surrender was accepted and Delshay along with 132 of his people were brought back to Camp Apache. It wasn't long after though that his band fled Camp Apache and returned to the Verde River where they remained peacefully for some months. In the late summer of that year it was said that Delshay was instigating an uprising among other Apache bands and, in response, Gen Crook ordered for Delshay's arrest. Before orders could be carried out however, Delshay and his band attacked the agency headquarters in the area and left the reservation -- heading down the Verde River for twenty miles before cutting off into the mountains. They weren't found until late October of that year; twnety-nine warriors were killed, nine prisoners captured, and while Delshay's brother was among the dead the cheif was still at large.

Of the four chiefs on Gen Crook's list, Delshay evaded capture the longest. He was killed in the summer of 1874. He was the last Apache chief in the Tonto Basin, his stronghold located south of present day Gisela at what is still known as Del Shay Basin. Following his death, there weren't any strong leaders in the area and any remaining members of his band either went into hiding or were forced to the reservations.

THE SCOOP

Red Ant is the center and original line on the wall.

(5.11 c/d) Follow jugs up the first few bolts to a rest ledge, from here the large holds disappear. Make your way through multiple thin cruxes, all with decent rests between them, until easier climbing at the top leads to the anchors. 14 bolts.

FA: Fishmans, Charlie Brown, Ross

THE SCOOP

(5.11b) An easy first few bolts leads to the technical crux -- five bolts of long reaches to perfect, incut edges -- then eases into a good rest. After you get a little back, blast up the last few bolts of easier but pumpy steep climbing to the anchors. 12 bolts.

FA: Julie Manello, Charlie Brown

BEAST WALL

The Beast Wall is a single-pitch wall slightly north of the main Hall. To get to the Beast Wall, park at a small pullout about a quarter mile from the main parking area at the end of the 4x4 road. Across the road you'll see the start of the trail up the hill. Follow the trail towards the big saguaro before it cuts across the gulley and towards the steep, south-facing wall.

GAAGE 38

Gaagé is the Apache word for raven.

THE SCOOP

The furthest left route on the wall. Stands slightly alone on a shorter tower that protrudes from the main part of the wall.

(5.11d) A steep start to hard climbing for the first two bolts. Then, follow easier terrain up and left for a few bolts before moving right around the arete back onto the face (clip the bolts out right before transitioning out) and continue up the steep, bulging face through the crux to the anchors. 8 bolts.

FA: Unknown

MAI 39

Mai is the Apache word for coyote.

THE SCOOP

Starts slightly up the hill from Gaage.

(5.9) A few bolts of juggy face climbing leads to a ledge below a chimney. The crux of the route is squeezing your way up the slighty bombay chimney. At the top of the chimney, step across to the hand crack and follow it up to the anchors. 12 bolts.

FA: Charlie Brown, Cas Sundell

BA'CHO 40

Ba'cho is the Apache word for wolf.

THE SCOOP

Third route from the left on the wall.

(5.11a) Start up easier terrain to a small ledge and a low, well-protected crux. Continue up the face on jugs out to the right of the bolt line to a mantle onto an airy ledge with a high clip. From here, thin holds and hard moves lead to the anchor.10 bolts.

FA: Unknown

THE SCORPION AND THE FROG 41

THE SCOOP

Starts further up the hill. The Scorpion and the Frog and Ni'tse are separated from the first three routes by a small pedestal of rock and a large, chossy crack on the face of the wall.

(5.10d) Start up the first two bolts of easy climbing to a small ledge before starting up the clean face. Fun moves on big holds following the crack to a large jug you can shake out on about three quarters of the way up the route. From here, move out left for a few bolts then continue up, trending right, to the anchors. 10 bolts.

FA: Charlie Brown, Cas Sundell

NI'TSE 42

Ni'tse is the Apache word for rattlesnake.

THE SCOOP

(5.12a) Start at a low bolt and continue up easy terrain to a rail. Hard moves off the rail lead to continuous climbing to a decent rest before the crux at the very top. 9 bolts.

FA: Charlie Brown, Cas Sundell

5.7

Net Positive Impact ☺
Do'a

5.8

Victorio ☺
Naiche's Escape
Jicarilla
Knotty Girl

5.9

Goyahkla ☺
Mischief Maker
Lipan
Yavapai
Coyotero
Chiricahua ☺
Mescalero
Knotty Tower
Mai

5.10B

Mangas ☺
Coloradas
Gouyen
Lozen
Ussen ☺

5.10C

Greatest Sin ☺
Apache Wolf
Níló

5.10D

Standing in Front of the Enemy ☺
Naiche
Black Hactcin
The Scorpion and the Frog

5.11A

White Hactcin
Ga'an ☺
Ba'cho

5.11B

Dahteste
Magazu
Wapotehe ☺

5.11C

Juh
Child of Water ☺
Red Ant

5.11D

Gaage

5.12A

Cochinay
Ni'tse

5.12B

Sons of Ussen ☺

5.12C

Slayer of Monsters ☺

REFERENCES

[1] "Our Culture". https://mescaleroapachetribe.com/our-culture/
[2] "Apache Before 1861". https://www.nps.gov/chir/learn/historyculture/pre-apache-wars.htm
[3] https://railsback.org/CS/CSCreation&Emergence.html

•Jacque J. Stewart. "The U.S. Government and the Apache Indians, 1871-1876: A Case Study in Counterinsurgency." Kutztown University, 1976.
•"Apache History in The Tonto Basin". https://discovergilacounty.com/blog-categories-gila-county-history/apache-history-in-the-tonto-basin/
•Jeffrey D. Carlisle. "The History and Culture of the Apache Indians," Handbook of Texas Online. https://www.tshaonline.org/handbook/entries/apache-indians
•Morris Edward Opler. "Myths and Tales of the Jicarilla Apache Indians: Memoirs of the American Folklore Society Vol. 31". Kraus Reprint Co., 1938.
•History.com Editors. "Chiricahua Apache Leader Victorio is Killed South of El Paso, Texas". https://www.history.com/this-day-in-history/october-15/chiricahua-apache-leader-victorio-is-killed-south-of-el-paso-texas. A&E Television Networks, 2009.
•Joseph A. Stout, Jr. "Victorio," Handbook of Texas Online. https://www.tshaonline.org/handbook/entries/victorio.
•Ruben Leyva. "Echos of Legacy: Apache Surnames, Survival, and Sovereignty". https://www.grantcountybeat.com/editorials/editorial/echoes-of-legacy-apache-surnames-survival-and-sovereignty.
•Jay Sharp. "The Night They Shot Mangas Coloradas". https://www.desertusa.com/ind1/Colradas.html.
•Eve Ball. *Indeh: An Apache Odyssey*. University of Oklahoma Press, 1988.
•"Apache Warrior Women". https://newmexiconomad.com/apache-warrior-women-gouyen-lozen-dahteste/.

PHOTOS

Charlie Brown (p 11, 15, 18, 19, 22, 27, 29)
Ian Gunn (p 17)
David Judkins (p 5, 6, 7, 12, 17)
Graham McNevin (p 8)
David Rozul (p 23)
Carrie Van Lanen (p 24)
Kim Wang (p 13)

Made in the USA
Coppell, TX
23 February 2026

72585808R00021